How to use this book

Follow the advice, in italics, given for you on each page.
Support the children as they read the text that is shaded in cream.
Praise *the children at every step!*

Detailed guidance is provided in the Read Write Inc. Phonics Handbook

9 reading activities

Children:
Practise reading the speed sounds.
Read the green, red and challenge words for the story.
Listen as you read the introduction.
Discuss the vocabulary check with you.
Read the story.
Re-read the story and discuss the 'questions to talk about'.
Read the story with fluency and expression.
Answer the questions to 'read and answer'.
Practise reading the speed words.

Speed sounds

Consonants *Say the pure sounds (do not add 'uh').*

f ff ph	l ll le	m mm (mb)	n nn kn	r rr wr	s ss se c ce	v ve	z zz (se) s	sh	th	ng nk

b bb	c k ck	d dd	g gg	h	j g ge	p pp	qu	t tt	w wh	x	y	ch tch

Vowels *Say the sounds in and out of order.*

at	hen head	in	on	up	day make	see tea happy	high smile lie find	blow home no

zoo brute blue	look	car	for door snore yawn	fair care	whirl nurse letter	shout cow	boy spoil

*Each box contains one sound but sometimes more than one grapheme. Focus graphemes are **circled**.*

Green words

cute   least   bowl   first   like   take   same   both   cage

girl   curl   turn   hurt   fur   her

heav`y   bod`y   a`lone

o`ver   pa`per   nev`er   to`geth`er   bett`er   suff`er   fing`er

scamp`er   af`ter   ham`ster   gin`ger   shel`ter   litt`er

re`mem`ber   prop`er   lay`er   scatt`er   corn`er   cov`er   sipp`er

use → used   bad-temper → bad-tempered

house → houses   sleep → sleepy   choose → choosing

discover → discovering   climb → climber   own → owner

big → bigger   thin → thinner

5

Red words

mother are you want to one your
they come other

Challenge words

eyes

Looking after a hamster

Introduction

Do you know what a hamster is?

If you were going to get a hamster – what kinds of information would you need to know so that you looked after him properly?

Find out all about hamsters and how to look after them. Read about what to put in their cage, what they like to play with, the food they like to eat and how to handle them.

Do you know how to check your hamster's health and what to do if it's sick? Find out here!

Story written by Gill Munton
Illustrated by Tim Archbold

Vocabulary check

Discuss the meaning (as used in the text) after the children have read each word.

	definition:	sentence/phrase:
ginger	pale orange colour	Hamsters are cute little animals with ginger fur.
animal shelter	place where animals are given good homes	You can get one from a pet shop or an animal shelter.
litter	a group of babies	A girl hamster can have a litter of pups when she is 10 weeks old.
peat	soil	Put a layer of peat on the floor.
scamper	run	Hamsters like to scamper about.

Punctuation to note in this text:
1. Capital letters to start sentences and full stop to end sentences
2. Capital letters for names

Looking after a hamster

Hamsters are cute little animals,

with ginger fur and long whiskers.

If you are an animal lover,

you may want to become the proud owner of a hamster.

You can get one from a pet shop or an animal shelter.

Choosing a hamster

A girl hamster can have a litter of pups

when she is 10 weeks old.

Your hamster must be at least 4–8 weeks old

before it leaves its mother.

Remember! Choose a hamster

with clean fur and bright eyes.

A home for your hamster

First, you will need a proper hamster cage – the bigger the better.

Put a layer of peat on the floor, and scatter wood shavings or shredded paper on top. When it is sleepy, your hamster will curl up in a corner and cover itself up.

Remember! Never keep hamsters together in the same cage – they will fight!

Hamster toys

Hamsters like to scamper about, discovering things to play with.

Get your hamster a hamster wheel.

Other toys can be made at home:

- tunnels made from loo roll tubes

- ladders made from bits of wood (hamsters are good climbers)

- little houses made from boxes.

Your hamster will also like to come out of its cage to play.
Scoop it up in both hands and hold it gently but firmly
next to your body.

Don't squeeze it –
it may bite your finger!

Pick it up each day –
it will soon get used to you.

Remember! Never leave a hamster alone in a room out of its cage.
It might get lost or hurt, or it might chew a bit of electric flex.

Feeding your hamster

Give your hamster:

- pellets (from the pet shop)
- bits of cornflake and bread
- currants, nuts and bits of cheese (for a treat)
- fresh, clean water (hamsters get thirsty, too!).

You will need a bowl to put the food in. It must be heavy so the hamster can't turn it over. A sipper tube is best for the water. Your hamster may stuff the food in its cheek pouches to eat later.

Remember! Take out stale food and dirt each day.

Clean the cage and change the bedding each week.

Keeping your hamster fit

Check your hamster each day.

Has it got a cold?

Is its bottom dirty?

Are its teeth or claws getting too long?

Is it getting thinner?

Is it bad-tempered?

Remember! Never let an animal suffer.

Take it to the vet if it is ill, so that he or she can make it better.

Questions to talk about

Re-read the page. Read the question to the children. Tell them whether it is a **FIND IT** *question or* **PROVE IT** *question.*

FIND IT

✓ *Turn to the page*

✓ *Read the question*

✓ *Find the answer*

PROVE IT

✓ *Turn to the page*

✓ *Read the question*

✓ *Find your evidence*

✓ *Explain why*

Page 9:   FIND IT   *Where can you buy a hamster from?*

Page 10:   PROVE IT   *Why do you think 'Remember! Choose a hamster with clean fur and bright eyes.' is written in bold?*

Page 11:   FIND IT   *How do you prepare the hamster's cage?*

Page 12:   PROVE IT   *What toys can you make for your hamster? Why do you think they like tunnels?*

Page 13:   FIND IT   *How should you hold your hamster? Why should you pick it up each day?*

Page 14:   PROVE IT   *What do hamsters eat? Why do you think hamsters stuff food in their cheek pouches to eat later?*

Page 15:   FIND IT   *How can you check your hamster is healthy?*

Questions to read and answer

(Children complete without your help.)

1. Where can you get a hamster from?

2. What do you need to buy for your hamster? (Make a list)

3. What can you make hamster toys from?

4. Why does it say **'Remember!...'** on every page?

5. How can you tell if your hamster is ill?

Speed words

Children practise reading the words across the rows, down the columns and in and out of order clearly and quickly.

choosing	body	heavy	leaves	alone
used	hurt	curl	later	paper
never	remember	after	discovering	become
don't	any	couldn't	where	behind